Unit 6

Lesson 26

Houghton
Mifflin
Harcourt

Reading Adventures

Welcome, Reader!

In this magazine you will read about animals from the distant past and from right now, including a fish that lives in both times! You'll explore a cave of crystals, a palace in a cliff, and a prehistoric tar pit (don't get too close).

You'll read poems and stories about fossils and mysterious deer, and travel even farther in a lot of fun activities.

Your journey to discovery begins when you turn the page!

"The Whale" from *Beast Feast* by Douglas Florian. Copyright © 1994 Douglas Florian. Reprinted by permission of Houghton Mifflin Harcourt Publishing Company. "Wild Geese" from *Bicycle Riding and Other Poems* by Sandra Olson Liatsos. Text copyright © 1997 by Sandra Olson Liatsos. Reprinted by permission of the author c/o Marian Reiner, Literary Agent. "Places and Names: A Traveler's Guide" from *A World of Wonders: Geographic Travels in Verse and Rhyme* by J. Patrick Lewis. Text copyright © 2002 by J. Patrick Lewis. Reprinted by permission of Dial Books for Young Readers, A Division of Penguin Young Readers Group, A Member of Penguin Group (USA) Inc., 345 Hudson Street, New York, NY 10014, and Curtis Brown Ltd. All rights reserved. "Books" from *Angels Ride Bikes and Other Fall Poems/ Los Angeles Andan en Bicicleta: Y Otros Poemas de Otoño* by Francisco X. Alarcón. Text copyright © 1999 by Francisco X. Alarcón. Reprinted by permission of Children's Book Press, San Francisco, CA, www. childrensbookpress.org. "Fossils" from *Something New Begins* by Lilian Moore. Copyright © 1973, 1982 by Lilian Moore. Reprinted by permission of the author c/o Marian Reiner, Literary Agent. "Deep in the forest..." from *Echoes for the Eye: Poems to Celebrate Patterns in Nature* by Barbara Juster Esbensen. Text copyright © 1996 by Barbara Juster Esbensen. Reprinted by permission of HarperCollins Publishers. "The Best Paths" from *Toasting Marshmallows: Camping Poems* by Kristine O'Connell George. Text copyright © 2001 by Kristine O'Connell George. Reprinted by permission of Houghton Mifflin Harcourt Publishing Company and the author. "compass" from *All The Small Poems and Fourteen More* by Valerie Worth. Text copyright © 1994 Valerie Worth. Reprinted by permission of Farrar, Straus & Giroux LLC. "Encounter" from *Something New Begins* by Lilian Moore. Copyright © 1973, 1982 by Lilian Moore. Reprinted by permission of the author c/o Marian Reiner, Literary Agent. "Journey of the Woolly Mammoth" by Maria Fleming. Copyright © Maria Fleming. Reprinted by permission of the author.

2014 Edition
Copyright © by Houghton Mifflin Harcourt Publishing Company

Printed in the U.S.A.

ISBN: 978-0-547-86583-6

7 8 9 10-0914-21 20 19 18 17 16 15 14 13   4500435331

Skywoman's Rescue

> **Setting:**
> *The dark, watery world below the sky*
>
> **Characters**
> *Narrator • Turtle • Toad • Otter*
> *Goose 1 • Goose 2 • Skywoman*

Narrator: The animals living below the sky led a peaceful life.

Toad: *(Lazily)* Should I swim, or should I take a nap? I'll nap.

Narrator: But one day two Geese flew down with news.

Goose 1: *(Landing in the water)* Guess what! Skywoman dreamed about a hole in the clouds! And her dream inspired the Chief to uproot the Great Tree!

Toad: Too bad. I liked that tree.

Goose 2: Now there really is a hole in the clouds!

Otter: *(Peering upward)* And Skywoman must have fallen through, because here she comes!

Turtle: Geese! Can you fly up and catch her?

Geese: We can—and we will! *(They fly off.)*

Narrator: While the Geese took off into the sky, Turtle thought about what to do next.

Turtle: Skywoman will need someplace to land. I doubt if she can swim.

Narrator: Turtle tilted her head, pondering. Finally she came to a decision.

Turtle: Toad! Swim down and bring up lots of mud!

Toad: Mud? That's your plan?

Turtle: As much mud as you can carry! Hurry!

Narrator: Toad dove into the water. Meanwhile, the Geese circled lower and lower with Skywoman between their wings. At last, Toad came to the surface. His mouth bulged with mud.

Turtle: Good! Now, you and Otter spread the mud over my shell, good and thick!

Otter: *(Spreading mud)* This will make a nice soft landing.

Narrator: Just in time, the Geese came down on Turtle's back with Skywoman.

Skywoman: Thank you, noble animals. You rescued me!

Toad: No problem. Hey, you have seeds!

Skywoman: Yes, I grabbed them from the Great Tree as I fell. *(She scatters the seeds on the mud.)*

Narrator: The seeds took root. Soon the mud became the earth, thick with plants and full of new life. And later, Skywoman gave birth to twins. They became the first people.

Toad: All because of me! *(Toad exits with a splash.)*

Leaving Home

On a warm summer day, a tiny striped fish wiggles out of the gravel of a riverbed in Northern California. For the next few months this young Pacific salmon, called a fry, explores the section of the river where she was born, feeding on insects and plants. Then instinct, knowledge she was born with, tells her to swim downstream. Tumbling over rocks and through rapids, the salmon finally reaches the mouth of the river, where it meets the sea. Saltwater and freshwater mix and the salmon spends a few weeks feeding on small shellfish as she doubles in size, loses her stripes, and turns a shining silver.

Then the young salmon travels out to sea, swimming for thousands of miles into the ocean. In a few years she will find her way back across the ocean and up the river to the exact section where she was born. How can she do this?

Animals have five senses, just as people do: sight, hearing, touch, taste, and smell. To navigate, they use these senses and other abilities that people don't have, such as echolocation, in ways that scientists are still trying to understand.

These sockeye salmon are returning to their home to spawn, or lay eggs.

The Move

Elephant Talk

Elephants trumpet when they are excited or alarmed. Mother elephants hum to their newborn babies. But people who study elephants have noticed something odd. A herd might be grazing peacefully in the African grasslands. Suddenly they all lift their heads, flap their ears, and begin to walk together in the same direction. They may walk for miles and then meet another herd. The elephants greet each other with loud trumpeting calls, flapping their ears and twisting their trunks together. It's a gigantic family reunion.

How did they find each other?

The elephants didn't see each other. If the wind was not blowing the right way, their sense of smell didn't help them. Scientists were puzzled. Dr. Katy Payne solved the puzzle when she recorded elephant sounds at a slow speed. She listened to the tapes at normal speed and heard elephant sounds no human had ever heard before. They were deep rumbles, too low for our ears to hear. But elephants could hear them from miles away. Scientists call this *infrasound*.

Sound moves in waves through the air. Low sounds like the elephants' rumbles move in long waves that can travel many miles. So elephants rumble back and forth to find each other.

Elephants travel together in groups across the African plains. They follow infrasonic calls their relatives make, sounds too low for human ears.

Why Bats Squeak

Bats also make sounds that humans cannot hear. But these sounds are not rumbles. They are high-pitched squeaks. Bats use these squeaks and their excellent hearing to find their way in the dark. They do so through *echolocation*, using echoes to locate something.

If you make a loud sound in a large, empty room, you will hear that sound come back to you as an echo. Echoes are created when sound waves move through the air, hit something, and bounce back. All sounds move in this way, bouncing back if they hit a solid object. But human hearing is not good enough to hear most echoes.

Bats, however, do hear these echoes. Bats make their squeaking sounds as they fly through the dark in search of food. The squeaks bounce off trees, houses, and other objects. This is useful in finding prey because echoes even bounce off insects! Amazingly, these bouncing echoes tell bats how far away the insect is, which direction it is moving, and how fast it is flying. Bats can even tell how fat and juicy the insect is! Echolocation is important to bats, because insects are their main source of food.

Sound waves from a bat's squeak bounce off an insect and travel back to the bat as an echo. In this way bats can find their dinner.

Why Bees Sing and Dance

Honeybees work together in a hive. Young bees work inside the hive. Older bees go outside to gather pollen and nectar from flowers to make honey. At first they make dozens of short flights to learn the lay of the land. Next, they learn the direction the sun appears to move. Finally, they fly as far as three miles from their hive to gather pollen.

Bees use their sense of smell as well as eyesight to find flowers. They use the sun to find their way home. On cloudy days, they look for landmarks they have learned. Back at the hive, they offer nectar they found to the other bees. Then the bees dance. Sometimes they move in circles. At other times, they zigzag or "waggle."

Beekeepers have long known that bees dance, but it was not until 1947 that scientists discovered why. When honeybees dance, they are telling the other bees where to find food. Researchers also discovered that the sounds bees make while dancing give information about finding flowers. The bees need the whole song and dance routine to learn how to return to the flowers and get nectar, too.

A honeybee's circular dance means flowers are nearby. A waggle dance signals that the flowers are farther away.

Bird Maps and Compasses

It is easy to get to places you've been to many times before. But traveling a long distance or an unknown route takes more planning. A map and a compass are often helpful for such trips. The map shows you how to get from one place to another. The compass can tell you in what direction you are moving.

Every year hundreds of species of birds take long trips, too. They fly hundreds and thousands of miles from one home to another. In the fall, they fly to warmer climates where food is plentiful all winter. When spring comes, they fly back to raise their young where they were born. For a long time people wondered where the birds went and what routes they took.

A crane in flight.

Researchers now know that migrating birds, such as cranes, are guided by their own sorts of maps and compasses. But it has taken many decades to uncover the secrets of these navigation tools. In the 1800s, scientists started putting bands around birds' legs. The bands contained a name and address. When people found the banded birds, they contacted the person named on the band and told that tracker where and when they had found the bird. In this simple way, scientists learned a lot about where birds traveled, where they stopped, and how fast they moved.

Today scientists still put light aluminum bands on birds' legs. They also use new ways of tracking birds—airplanes, computers, tiny radio transmitters, and satellites. Scientists have answered many questions about how birds navigate.

Endangered whooping cranes learn a migration route by following an ultralight aircraft.

Some birds migrate in a flock. You may have seen Canada geese flying high in the sky in the form of a V. Young birds follow their parents and learn the route that the older geese have traveled before. They may follow a river and remember what it looks like. Certain sounds or smells will stay in their memory. Also, like captains on sailing ships long ago, birds use the position of the sun and stars as a compass to find their way.

Birds and many other animals also use earth's magnetic field to navigate. Chemicals in these animals' brains allow them to sense the magnetic field and travel in the right direction. But scientists are still researching how this happens. They think some birds may actually be able to see earth's magnetic field.

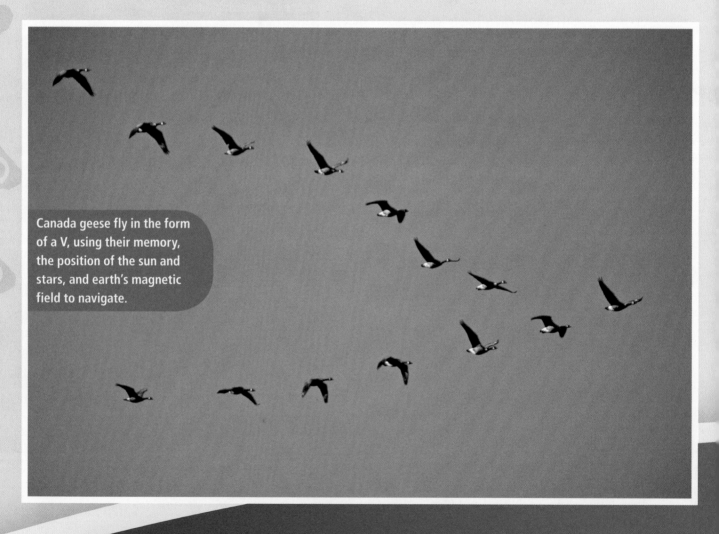

Canada geese fly in the form of a V, using their memory, the position of the sun and stars, and earth's magnetic field to navigate.

Returning Home

After leaving the river, the Pacific salmon lives in the ocean for the next few years. Eventually, though, she begins her return journey. She is going home to the stream where she was born to lay eggs, or spawn. How does a salmon remember the route she took years before and find her way back?

Scientists don't know all the answers, but here's what they think is happening: a Pacific salmon feels the temperature of the water and the ocean currents. She tastes how the saltiness of the water changes in different places. She sees the location of the sun and the star patterns at night. Like a migrating bird, she can sense the earth's magnetic field to find her way.

Finally, the salmon remembers the smell of her birthplace. The plants that grow and the leaves that fall from the trees create a special odor for each stream.

She swims up over the rocks and rapids on her last journey. She will lay eggs to create the next generation of Pacific salmon. Then she will die, leaving her fry to make their own journeys using instinct and navigation skills they inherit from their parents.

Each year, thousands of salmon return to the waters where they hatched. They use many clues to find their way back.

The Whale

by Douglas Florian

Big as a street —

With fins, not feet —

I'm full of blubber,

With skin like rubber.

When I breathe out,

I **spew** a spout.

I swim by the shore

And eat more and more.

I'm very, very hard to ignore.

14

Wild Geese

by Sandra Olson Liatsos

When I watch
Their flock in flight
And when I hear their cries
I wonder how
They always know
Their way through
Distant skies.

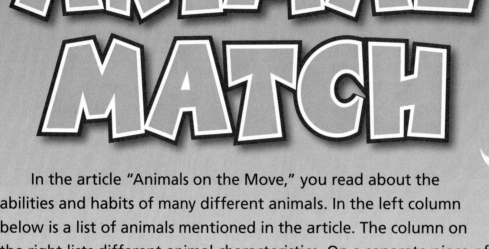

ANIMAL MATCH

In the article "Animals on the Move," you read about the abilities and habits of many different animals. In the left column below is a list of animals mentioned in the article. The column on the right lists different animal characteristics. On a separate piece of paper, match each description to the animal it describes best. Review the article if you're not sure!

1. Salmon
2. Elephant
3. Bat
4. Honeybee

A. makes a rumbling sound that people cannot hear
B. moves in a zigzag motion
C. returns to its place of birth to spawn
D. uses high-pitched squeaks to find its way

WILD SIMILES

Similes are comparisons that use the word *like* or *as*. A simile helps people understand something by comparing it to something else. In the poem "The Whale," for example, the whale says that it is as "Big as a street... With skin like rubber."

Create two or three similes about an animal mentioned in "Animals on the Move" or about an animal of your choice. Use features from the chart below. Take turns reading your similes with a partner.

Feature	Example
size	as tall as a tree
texture	as smooth as glass
movement	racing like the wind
color	as black as ink
sound	cooing like a flute

Wild

In "Animals on the Move" you read about how salmon, bats, bees, birds, and elephants travel. You read how they use their five senses. You also learned about special abilities they have, such as echolocation, the waggle dance, and steering by earth's magnetic field.

Choose an animal from the article or another animal you know about. Write a story about an adventure it has while traveling.

Traveler

Use a story map to plan the setting and the plot, including a problem and solution. Does the animal get lost? Is it trying to get home? Does it escape from danger?

As you write, include dialogue. Maybe human characters in your story talk about the animal. Maybe one animal speaks to another. Dialogue is a good way of developing the plot of a story.

There have been many books written about animals that go on journeys. *Lassie Come-Home*, by Eric Knight, is about a collie that makes a long and difficult journey home after being separated from its master. *The Black Stallion*, by Walter Farley, tells the tale of a beautiful black horse that is shipwrecked on a desert island with a boy named Alec.

Another well-read animal adventure is *The Incredible Journey* by Sheila Burnford. A Labrador retriever, a bull terrier, and a Siamese cat face many obstacles on a journey of two hundred miles before returning home.

Your story may become the next classic!

Mysteries at Cliff Palace

Cast of Characters

Narrator
Ruben
Rosa
Mom
Dad
Ranger Jenkins

Narrator: Ten-year-old Ruben, his older sister Rosa, and their parents are visiting Mesa Verde National Park in Colorado. They're with a group waiting for a ranger-guided tour of the cliff dwellings.

Ruben: Wow, this is going to be great! I'm going to solve one of the great mysteries of ancient North America, with the help of my trusty notebook!

Mom: Just look how many dwellings are built into the cliff alcove down there!

Ruben: All those walls and towers inside the ledge are really cool!

Mom: This was all built by the Ancestral Puebloan people.

Dad: That's right. These dwellings have been here about 800 years.

Ruben: I can't wait to see Cliff Palace up close. I'm sure I can find some clues to the mystery of why the people all disappeared.

Rosa: Right, Ruben. You can't even keep track of your lucky pen. So how can you solve a real mystery?

Ruben: Don't remind me, Rosa. I looked all over the car for it.

Dad: Hey, Ruben, here comes the ranger.

Mom: I bet she knows a lot about the Puebloan mystery.

Narrator: Ranger Jenkins arrives and introduces herself.

Ranger Jenkins: Gather round, everyone. We'll be descending 100 feet into the canyon. It's quite a trek, so be prepared.

Ruben: Aren't there five eight-foot ladders to climb?

Ranger Jenkins: It's challenging, but you can do it.

Rosa (to Ruben): I hope I can. It's so hot!

Ruben: I'll push you along if you need it. Just promise you'll tell me if you find any clues to the mystery.

Dad: Rosa, didn't you have a question for Ranger Jenkins?

Rosa: Yes! Why is this park named Mesa Verde? Doesn't that mean "green table" in Spanish?

Ranger Jenkins: Exactly! You see these huge, flat hills all around us? They're sometimes called plateaus. But they're as flat as tabletops, so they're also called mesas. And *verde* just refers to all the green plants and trees growing here.

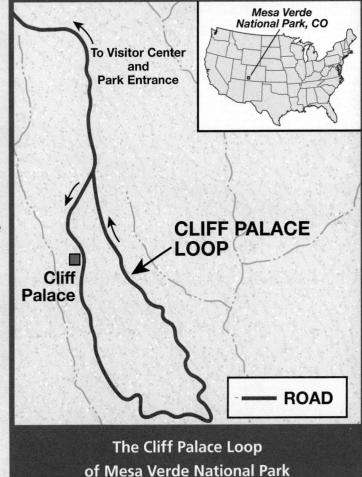

The Cliff Palace Loop
of Mesa Verde National Park

21

Narrator: Ruben waves his hand urgently.

Ruben: I've been reading a lot about the Ancestral Puebloans who built these cities like Cliff Palace. I read that at some time they just left here, and I'm trying to figure out why.

Ranger Jenkins: Great question, Ruben. Historians have been puzzling over this mystery for a long time. I'd like to hear your ideas.

Ruben: Well... I'm not sure, but—

Rosa: What *I* want to know is how they built those dwellings.

Ranger Jenkins: We'll talk a bit about that during the tour, Rosa. Okay, did everyone see the alcoves in the canyon walls? These cliffs are made of sandstone and shale, and sandstone is soft—it easily breaks and crumbles away. Over time, that breaking and crumbling carved the alcoves out of the rock.

Dad: So when did the Ancestral Puebloans start living here?

Ranger Jenkins: They came to this area around 600 C.E., but it wasn't until around 1200 that they built these dwellings in the cliffs. Let's go take a closer look at their handiwork. Watch where you're walking, everyone. The steps down are really rough and uneven.

Narrator: Ruben doesn't notice he's dropped his notebook on the steps. His mother hands it to him, and then goes on ahead to take pictures.

Dad: How about that pen you were missing, Ruben? Did you find it yet?

Ruben: I don't know where it went, Dad! It's not in any of my pockets.

Rosa: See, I told you. How can he solve an ancient mystery? He can't even solve the mystery of his missing stuff!

Ruben: Dad, tell Rosa to stop teasing! In fact—I bet she has my pen.

Rosa: I do not!

Dad: What does it look like?

Ruben: It has a digital thermometer on it, so I can tell the temperature! I always use it when I take tests.

Ranger Jenkins: Listen up, everyone. This round pit in front of us is called a *kiva*. A kiva is a ceremonial room. The Ancestral Puebloans built kivas for special religious ceremonies. If you look over there, you can see where the people climbed up the cliffs to the top of the mesa farm. And of course, this is Cliff Palace. Cliff Palace has twenty-three kivas and 150 rooms, which housed about 100 people, we think.

Ruben: Man, look at all these cliff dwellings!

Dad: And those towers. Just think of the work that went into building all this!

Ruben: Yeah, but the people only lived here for around 75 to 100 years. Why would they just leave?

Rosa: Maybe they were thirsty, like me. It is so hot here! And I already drank all my water.

Ruben: Hey, you could be right, Rosa! There was a drought here, sometime, wasn't there?

Ranger Jenkins: Yes, there was! The drought began in 1276 and may have lasted for twenty years. A lot of people think that Ancestral Puebloans left after their crops died and they didn't have enough food.

On the other hand, the people had survived droughts in the past. They stored food to prepare for hard times. Why would this drought drive them away if they had survived others?

Ruben: Don't some people think maybe a war forced them to leave?

Ranger Jenkins: Right, there may have been a war. It might have started with one group raiding another for food.

Ruben: Or maybe the different groups fought for each other's land, to get the best places to grow crops and find water.

Narrator: After discussing their ideas with Ranger Jenkins, Ruben decides to look for clues.

Mom: Ruben, did you see where Rosa went?

Ruben: Mom! All these dwellings are made of sandstone bricks. The Puebloans made them one by one—by hand! So why leave after all that work?

Dad: It's great that you're keeping notes on this mystery, Ruben. But you didn't see Rosa wander off?

Ruben: Wait—my notebook! Dad, I lost it again!

Mom: We'll look for your notebook, Ruben, once we find Rosa.

Dad: I'll go see if she's with that group over there.

Ranger Jenkins: It's almost time to go. Take a few more minutes to look around, and then we'll climb those ladders up the cliff.

Mom: Quick, let's check all around the dwellings.

Narrator: Ruben looks around. He finds Rosa sitting in the shade of a rock wall near one of the Cliff Palace dwellings.

Ruben: What are you doing way over here, Rosa?

Rosa: Looking for shade! I was really hot and tired. I just needed to get out of the sun.

Ruben: You should have told Mom where you were going.

Rosa: I know. I was just going to sit here for a minute. But then I started looking at these cool bricks. And I started thinking how terrible it must have been to have no water here!

Ruben: That *could* be why the Ancestral Puebloans left, even though they worked so hard to build this city.

Rosa: So you haven't found out the reason for sure? Now I'm really wondering about it, too.

Ruben: No. And my notebook's lost again.

Rosa: Here it is. You left it by a tower, so I picked it up for you.

Ruben: Great! Do you have my pen, too?

Rosa: I promise I do not have your pen, Ruben. I wish I did. Then I could see exactly how hot it is out here! But being here makes me want to help solve this mystery.

Ruben: Good. But we'd better get back. It's almost time to go.

Narrator: Rosa and Ruben return to the group. Their parents are happy to see Rosa safe. The tour is about to end.

Ranger Jenkins: So, Ruben. Before we go, have you solved the mystery of the Ancestral Puebloans?

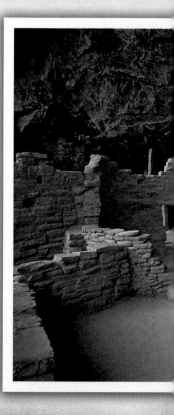

Ruben: Nope. But at least I have a few theories.

Mom: Okay, I'm ready to climb this ladder.

Ruben: Wait! Hold on, Mom! What's that sticking out of your back pocket?

Rosa: Oh, my gosh!

Ruben: Looks like a digital thermometer. It's my lucky pen!

Mom: Goodness, this thing? I found it on the ground near our car after we got here. I had no idea it was yours, Ruben. Here you go!

Dad: Well, we solved the mysteries of the lost Rosa, the lost notebook, and the lost pen today. Not bad for one day's work.

Ruben: Yeah, and now that I have my lucky pen back, I might solve the Ancestral Puebloans mystery in a few years!

Ranger Jenkins: With some good research, you just might! Now, everybody—up we go!

CAVE OF THE CRYSTALS

Imagine yourself one thousand feet underground, drilling a new tunnel in an old zinc and lead mine. Suddenly your drill bursts through the rock wall. What you see takes your breath away. Huge crystals fill a cave from end to end, floor to ceiling. They shimmer like moonlight. But before you can explore the cave, you are hit with air as hot as a blast from a furnace.

Two mineworkers, Juan and Pedro Sanchez, discovered this amazing "Cave of the Crystals" in 2000 at the Naica Mine in the state of Chihuahua, Mexico. They didn't stay long, for the intense heat drove them away.

The mine owners put an iron door at the mouth of the cave. Scientists came to study the cave, but because of the heat, they could stay inside for only a few minutes at a time.

The Cave of the Crystals is located in the desert of northern Mexico.

Inside Mexico's Cave of the Crystals

Scientists found the crystals were made of selenite gypsum, a translucent, light-colored mineral. The cave had just the right combination of minerals, water, and temperature to grow the crystals. The cave had once been filled with water, and heat from the earth's core kept the water at about 136 degrees Fahrenheit. This heated water caused some of the crystals to grow 36 feet long, about as tall as a three-story house! These are some of the largest natural crystals ever found.

Another team of scientists is now exploring the whole cave, which is nearly as large as a basketball court. They had to invent special clothing and breathing equipment for their work. Now they can stay inside for up to an hour at a time.

Water pumps keep the Naica Mine from filling with water. But without water the crystals will not grow any larger. Should the owners stop pumping out the water, so that the caves will flood again and the crystals will grow even larger? Or should they keep on pumping out the water, so that people can visit the cave? What would you do?

It took hundreds of thousands of years for the 36-foot crystals to get that big.

Places and Names: A Traveler's Guide

By J. Patrick Lewis

So many places have fabulous names,
Like Fried, North Dakota,
The Court of St. James,
Siberia, Nigeria, Elyria, Peru,
The White Nile, Black Sea,
And Kalamazoo!
The Great Wall of China, South Pole and Loch Ness,
And 104 Fairview—that's my address!

Thousands of spaces are places to be—
Discover the World of GE-OG-RA-PHY!

Travel by boat or by car or by plane
To visit East Africa, Singapore, Spain.
Go by yourself or invite a good friend,
But traveling by poem is what I recommend.

Los libros

Books

By Francisco X. Alarcón

pasaportes
de talla mayor

que nos permiten
viajar

a dondequiera
cuandoquiera

y no dejar
de soñar

oversized
passports

that let us
travel

anywhere
anytime

and keep on
dreaming

Think about Ruben, Rosa, and Ranger Jenkins in "Mysteries at Cliff Palace." Each one shows special personality traits. Read the traits below. Then match each one to the character who best shows that trait.

a knowledgeable

b curious

c teasing

d forgetful

e helpful

How does each trait contribute to the character's role in the story?

On a sheet of paper, draw a comic strip. Show characters' traits through their words.

Sensing the Cave

Imagine a hike to the Cave of the Crystals or another kind of cave. Think about the details your five senses would give you. On a separate sheet of paper, make a word web like the one on this page. Fill in each oval with sensory details for that sense. Below are two examples.

Use your web to write a description of your hike. A description can include an idiom, a phrase whose meaning is different from the meanings of its words. Think about the idiom "takes your breath away" in the first paragraph of "Cave of the Crystals." Discuss with a partner what that phrase means.

Bon Voyage!

Hawaii

Egypt

Hawaii? Egypt? The South Pole? Travel brochures are a great way to learn about places you've never visited. They give you a lot of details so you can imagine what a visit there would be like. Would you like to go to Mesa Verde National Park? Are you ready to explore the Cave of the Crystals? Or is there some other place you've visited that you really enjoyed?

Create a travel brochure about one of these places. Use details from "Mysteries at Cliff Palace" or "Cave of the Crystals" if you choose to write about either of these. If you write about someplace else, try to remember the most interesting details about that place.

South Pole

To start, fold a piece of letter-sized paper in half or in thirds. This will give your brochure a cover and some places inside for information. Title your brochure and make the cover colorful and interesting. Inside, give your readers details that would make them want to visit. Remember to write in a way that uses all the senses. If you paint a picture with words, your readers will easily imagine the place—and they'll want to visit it themselves!

To help you as you write, think about these questions:

What is unique about the destination?

What is the weather like?

What kinds of activities are offered?

Will visitors need special clothing?

Where can visitors stay?

Finally, draw pictures or cut out photos from magazines to illustrate your brochure. Bon voyage!

FOSSILS
A Peek Into the Past

Big news came out of Fairbanks, Alaska, in the fall of 2007. A ten-year-old boy named Jared Post had made a fantastic find. While walking home from school, Jared noticed a big, jagged rock half buried in the ground. Instantly curious, he dug the rock out. He noticed that it had what he called "weird engravings" on its underside. Jared felt pretty sure he had found something special—a fossil.

The young student's hunch was right. After bringing the toaster-sized object home, Jared and his dad searched the Internet for information. They discovered that the strange "rock" was in fact the tooth of a woolly mammoth, a giant mammal that lived during the Ice Age. The Ice Age occurred between 1.6 million and 10,000 years ago. In other words, that tooth was old!

The huge mammoth tooth Jared Post found weighed seven pounds. Jared is deciding whether to keep the tooth or donate it to a museum.

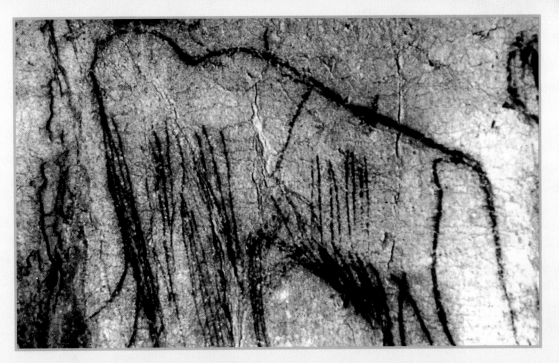

This drawing of a woolly mammoth was found on a cave wall in France.

Traces of the Past

Today, mammoths are extinct, meaning they no longer exist. Scientists can learn about them only by studying whatever remains they can find, such as bones, tusks, and teeth.

Animal teeth give a lot of information. By studying teeth, scientists can make a good guess about an animal's diet. Carnivores, or meat-eating animals, have sharp canine teeth to stab and hold on to prey. Herbivores are plant eaters, so they have large molars for chewing plants.

Although mammoths roamed throughout much of North America, Europe, Asia, and Africa, their bones and teeth are found mainly in areas with very cold weather. Any ideas why? It's because bones and teeth buried in frozen ground are less likely to be damaged. It's not surprising that Jared's mammoth tooth lasted 10,000 years or more. In his hometown of Fairbanks, the temperature stays below freezing more than half the year!

The pointed teeth of carnivores are much different than herbivore teeth.

Imagine a Woolly Mammoth!

For about two million years, woolly mammoths roamed the northern plains of Europe, North America, and Asia. Then, about 10,000 years ago, they disappeared, leaving only fossilized clues to their presence.

Thought to be early ancestors of today's elephants, these giant beasts were covered in dense shaggy hair. A thick layer of fat protected them from the cold. Teeth such as the one Jared discovered, probably a molar, indicates they were grass and leaf eaters. They used their long curving tusks, scientists believe, to shovel snow off the ground to reach buried plants.

Mammoths weighed about six to eight tons and stood about nine feet tall. Imagine an animal standing about as high as a one-story house and weighing as much as three or four full-sized pickup trucks.

"Just thinking about mammoths walking around my neighborhood 10,000 years ago is amazing!" Jared Post told reporters.

Fossils have given us most of the clues about the woolly mammoth.

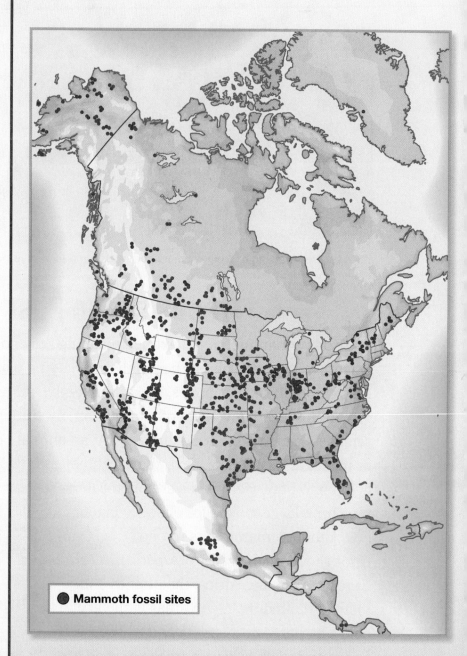

● Mammoth fossil sites

Dots on this map show some of the major North American sites where mammoth fossils have been found.

One Girl's Remarkable Finds

Another super-successful young fossil hunter was Mary Anning, who was born on the south coast of England. Mary got quite a head start on recent fossil finders. She discovered the skeleton of a giant sea creature when she was about eleven years old. That was in 1810!

Scientists had never seen anything like the bones Mary found. They named it *ichthyosaurus* (ick thee oh SOR us), from the Greek words for fish and lizard. But it was not a fish at all. Later research proved it to be the fossilized body of a giant sea reptile.

Mary got credit for finding the very first ichthyosaur fossil. But she discovered others as well. In 1821, she found two—one five feet long and the other almost twenty feet long. These discoveries started a fossil craze in England.

Three-year-old Kaleb Kidd in La Crosse, Wisconsin, holds the woolly mammoth tooth he found.

A Very Good Year

Jared wasn't the only young discoverer to come across a mammoth's tooth in 2007. It was a great year for finds! In February, 16-year-old Sierra Sarti-Sweeney found a tooth in Tampa, Florida. And in November, little Kaleb Kidd discovered a mammoth tooth in La Crosse, Wisconsin. At three years old, Kaleb might be the youngest fossil finder ever!

Nature's Memory Keepers

A fossil is the remains of a plant or an animal that lived a long time ago.

The word "fossil" was first used in the 1500s. It comes from a Latin word that means "dug up from the ground." The most common kind of fossil is an imprint, or outline, of the plant or animal in a rock. These kinds of fossils are formed in much the same way as a handprint in clay. Other kinds of fossils include animal bones and footprints, or even a trail left by a worm.

Fossils might be called nature's memory keepers because they show what once was. They are little—or sometimes big—pieces of history. Because fossils give us clues about extinct plants and animals, they help us understand what the world was like in the distant past.

Fossil of a wading bird found in Wyoming

The coastal area where Mary lived was, and still is, full of fossils. Most of these are the remains of animals that lived in the seas between 206 and 144 million years ago, a time known as the Jurassic period. The ichthyosaurus was from this time, when dinosaurs roamed the earth. But Mary was also the first to discover the remains of another Jurassic sea creature.

This skeleton, found in 1823, was equally large and strange. The fossil measured nine feet long and six feet wide. Compared to its giant body, its head was tiny—not quite five inches long! The creature was named Plesiosaurus, meaning "almost like a lizard."

Mary Anning's fossils gave scientists new knowledge about the world.

Mary learned her skills as a fossil hunter from her father. He showed her how to increase the value of her finds by cleaning them with a needle and a small brush, then polishing them. After her father died, Mary's sale of her fossil finds helped keep the family going. Her dedication to this work made her famous as an expert on fossils.

Because she was only a young girl, and not a trained scientist, Mary's knowledge of fossils was almost unbelievable to people of her time. One person wrote that Mary had the knowledge to easily talk with "professors and other clever men on the subject, and they all [admit] she understands more of the science than anyone else in the kingdom."

No wonder Mary Anning has been called "the greatest fossilist the world ever knew."

Plesiosaurus fossil

Trapped in Tar!

Walk down a paved black road on a hot summer day and you might find your shoes starting to sink in. That's because high heat makes the road surface soft. If this happens, you are probably walking on asphalt, or tar.

Luckily, you won't sink in very far. But 28,000 years ago, bubbling black asphalt deposits, or tar pits, swallowed up a great many unlucky animals. Possibly thinking they had found water, the mammoths or ground sloths blundered into pits of sticky, gooey tar. Instead of a drink or a bath, a trap held them fast, forever.

These same tar pits still bubble today—in the middle of Los Angeles, California, one of the largest American cities. But what was bad luck for prehistoric animals has meant good luck for paleontologists, scientists who study fossils.

Known as the Rancho La Brea Tar Pits, the bubbling pools of asphalt contain the remains of woolly mammoths, saber-toothed cats, giant sloths, and other now-extinct beasts. This makes the La Brea Tar Pits one of the world's richest sources of fossils.

Lifelike statues at the tar pits make it easy for visitors to imagine a mammoth's deadly dip. ▶

This skull of a saber-toothed cat, from the La Brea Tar Pits, is the only one ever found with its mouth closed.

Paleontologists at work at Los Angeles's Page Museum. ▼

The asphalt in these pits has been oozing from the ground for about 40,000 years, and more than three million fossils have been found. In addition to mammoths, tigers, and sloths, paleontologists have found the remains of horses, coyotes, wolves, bison, birds, rodents, and insects, many in perfect condition.

Today, the La Brea Tar Pits are part of Los Angeles's Page Museum, whose current hot spot is Pit 91. Paleontologists keep finding thousands of fossils in this pit under the watchful eyes of visitors.

After seeing complete animal skeletons and learning how the animals became trapped in tar, a visitor to the Rancho La Brea Tar Pits might feel lucky. Those animals met a fate much worse than leaving a shoe print behind on a black-topped road!

JOURNEY OF THE WOOLLY MAMMOTH

By Maria Fleming

On pillared legs, with tread of thunder,
you trudged across the endless tundra,
a mountain of fur, twin tusks thrust high,
back hunched beneath the weight of the sky.

Until you met some unknown doom,
disappeared into an icy tomb,
a secret buried underground,
ten thousand years lost . . .

Then found.

You walk again inside these walls,
a ghost that haunts museum halls.
Ice Age icon, here enshrined,
once frozen in earth,
now frozen in time.

Fossils

by Lilian Moore

Older than
books,
than scrolls,

older
than the first
tales told

or the
first words
spoken

are the stories

in the forests that
turned to
stone

in ice walls
that trapped the
mammoth

in the long
bones of
dinosaurs—

the fossil
stories that begin
Once upon a time

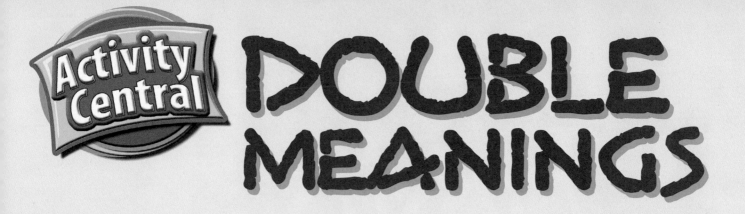

Activity Central
DOUBLE MEANINGS

Quick—what's a fossil? Is it A: the preserved evidence of a prehistoric plant or animal; or B: someone who has very old-fashioned ideas? Surprise—it's both!

Meaning A is *fossil*'s denotation, its factual meaning. Meaning B is its connotation, or an idea that is suggested by the word. Understanding the context of a sentence containing a word with multiple meanings can help you clarify what the word means.

Read the sentences below. Use the context of each sentence to help you decide if its meaning is a denotation (D) or connotation (C).

1. This mammoth's <u>woolly</u> hair is covered in tar.   __?__

2. Its thinking is confused and <u>woolly</u>.   __?__

3. How did it get into this <u>sticky</u> situation?   __?__

4. It is trapped in a pool of <u>sticky</u> asphalt.   __?__

5. The mammoth is in a <u>pit</u> of despair.   __?__

6. It never should have blundered into the <u>pit</u>.   __?__

Challenge: Make up two more sentences with multiple meanings for the words *wild* and *sharp*.

Prove It!

Half of these statements about fossils are facts. The others are opinions. Take turns reading the statements with a partner. Which are facts and which are opinions?

1. This shell fossil was found in Ithaca, New York.
   o Fact
   o Opinion

2. It would not be a good idea to try to saw petrified wood.
   o Fact
   o Opinion

3. This appears to be the bone of a stegosaurus.
   o Fact
   o Opinion

4. This ammonite fossil shows its coiled shape.
   o Fact
   o Opinion

5. This is the footprint of a terrifying dinosaur.
   o Fact
   o Opinion

6. This fern fossil has four fronds.
   o Fact
   o Opinion

YOUR OPINION COUNTS!

Fairbanks, Alaska

10-year-old Boy Finds 10,000-year-old Tooth!

Newspapers all over the world publish letters from their readers. People often write to offer their opinions about something they've read in the news.

You've read about Jared Post, who found the woolly mammoth tooth in Fairbanks, Alaska. After showing the tooth to scientists, Jared was unsure about whether he would keep it or not.

Suppose you read the story about Jared in a Fairbanks newspaper. Write a letter to the newspaper telling whether you think Jared should keep the tooth or donate it to a museum—and why you think so. If he keeps the tooth, what should he do with it? If he gives it up, who should get it, and why? Include facts, but focus on your opinion. Explain your reasons for your point of view. If you write a strong, persuasive letter, you might even change someone else's opinion—with help from the tips below.

Tips from the Experts

Do you want to get your letter to the editor published? Here are some pointers.

- **Be Brief.** Get right to the point.

- **Be Accurate.** Check your facts.

- **Be Polite.** Avoid insults.

- **Be Professional.** Remember to sign your letter. Include your name, address, and telephone number. If you e-mail your letter, be sure to include your full name, city, and state.

- **Be Patient.** If at first you don't succeed, keep trying.

Fossil Fish FOUND!

The year was 1938. A strange guest had found its way onboard the *Nerine*, a fishing boat sailing off the coast of South Africa. It was a huge fish with steel-blue eyes and a pale blue body with silver markings. The fishermen had never caught anything like it.

The fish acted strangely, too. It crawled slowly across the boat's deck on fins that looked like stubby legs. It oozed thick oil from its body, and bit the boat captain's hand. Then, about three hours after its capture, it died.

"Old Fourlegs," as the fishermen named it, had no value in the food market. But it was very unusual.

The captain called Marjorie Courtenay-Latimer, who sometimes displayed odd fish in her museum in East London, South Africa.

This was not just any old fish. It was a "living fossil" that caused a worldwide stir. Old Fourlegs turned out to be a *coelacanth* (SEE luh kanth), a fish that first lived about 400 million years ago. Until 1938, scientists had only seen fossils of this kind of fish. They believed it had been extinct for 70 million years!

Coelacanths are sometimes called dinofish because they were around even before dinosaurs.

The coelacanth's official name is *Latimeria chalumnae* in honor of Ms. Courtenay-Latimer.

Unable to identify it, Ms. Courtenay-Latimer wrote to a scientist named J.L.B. Smith. Dr. Smith, an expert on fish, was excited. It sounded to him like the lost coelacanth. By the time he managed to reach East London, the fish had been stuffed and its organs thrown away. Still, he could tell it was a coelacanth.

Dr. Smith spent the next fourteen years looking for another one. He put up posters in places all along Africa's east coast. He offered a cash reward to anyone who found one.

In 1952, Dr. Smith heard that fishermen in the Comoros Islands, near Madagascar, had caught a coelacanth. He rushed to see it and was surprised to learn that the men had caught this kind of fish before, but threw them back in the ocean because they were not good to eat.

Since the discovery of Old Fourlegs, a number of coelacanths have been found, but they are still rare. Many consider this fossil the "most important scientific discovery of the 1900s."

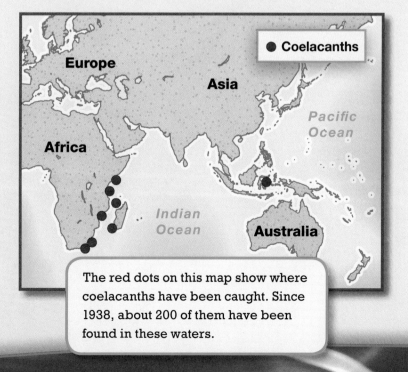

The red dots on this map show where coelacanths have been caught. Since 1938, about 200 of them have been found in these waters.

Fun Fact: Scientists believe the coelacanth can live up to 100 years.

The Case of the
Missing Deer

"Do you think we'll see some deer soon?" Blake asked.

From their chairs on the small patio, his mom and grandpa both nodded. The three had just arrived at their vacation cabin. Blake was kicking his soccer ball around the wide lawn that their cabin shared with three others. Beyond that were the woods, like a thick green wall. Grandpa had said the deer came right up to the cabins here, and Blake really hoped it was true.

"You'll have to wait until it cools off," Grandpa told him. "But I bet we'll see some this evening."

"Hey, pass me the ball!"

Blake looked up to see a girl about his age coming toward him from the next cabin. He kicked his soccer ball her way.

The girl trapped the ball with her foot. "I'm Maria," she said. "My family has been here three days, and this place is great. But I forgot my soccer ball." She pointed to a third cabin. "There are two brothers staying at that cabin, Nicholas and Todd. We've just been kicking a pinecone around the last couple days."

"I heard that the deer come right up to the cabins around here," Blake said.

"They do. It's really cool."

"All right! A real soccer ball!"

Two boys appeared from around the side of one of the cabins. It was Nicholas and his younger brother, Todd. Within minutes the four of them had a game going, with lawn chairs as goal posts.

The game was loud and rowdy. And even though it was late afternoon, the sun was still strong. Blake pulled his sweatshirt off and flung it on one of the chairs. After an hour of playing, and a few points scored by each team, they wrapped it up.

Maria called to Blake as the new friends all headed back to their own cabins and dinner.

"Hope you see the deer tonight!"

"Me, too!" Blake replied.

But no such luck. After dinner, Blake kept watch for a while at the glass door. When no deer appeared, he joined his family to watch a video. But he kept going to the windows to check. By bedtime, Blake had not caught sight of a single deer. Living in the city, he would never be able to see deer on his doorstep. This was his only chance!

The next day, Blake and his family had a lot of activities planned. But by late afternoon, he caught up again with Maria, Todd, and Nicholas. As they set up pinecones to dribble the soccer ball around, Todd said, "Did you see all the deer last night?"

"A mom and her babies were right outside our kitchen window!" Maria said.

"We didn't see any at all," Blake replied. "We thought maybe it was too cold."

"No way!" Nicholas said. "They were all over the place."

Blake frowned as he kicked the soccer ball across the lawn.

"I'm sure they'll come to your cabin, too, Blake," Maria assured him. "I saw them in your yard before you got here."

"I don't get it," Blake said the next day when he learned his friends had spotted deer in their yards again. Again, the animals had avoided Blake's cabin. What was everyone else doing right?

"Maybe I'll put some food out there. Like some apples," Blake decided. Nicholas, Todd, and Maria thought this might work.

54

Before dinner, Blake scattered apples near the cabin and all over the yard. He might not catch sight of a deer, but if the apples were eaten, at least he would know they had come to his cabin, too!

The next morning, Blake hurried outside to check on the apples. Not a single bit of apple had been eaten. It looked as if none of them had even been moved.

"It's the case of the missing deer," Todd said when Blake glumly reported his bad news later that afternoon.

"Sounds like a detective story," said Maria.

"One I want to solve!" Blake said. "I need to start thinking like a detective."

"That means starting with all the facts you already know," Nicholas replied.

There were many things the friends knew about the case of the missing deer. They wrote down what cabins the deer went to and when, as well as how many they had seen.

"Are you sure you saw deer around our cabin before we got here?" Blake asked Maria.

Maria's Cabin? YES
Nicholas's Cabin? YES
Blake's Cabin? No

She nodded. "Definitely."

"Could it be the soccer ball?" Nicholas asked. "Before you got here, we didn't have one. Maybe the sound bothers the deer."

"But they don't come out at the time of day when we play. At night, it's quiet. So it can't be that."

A search around the cabins provided no clues either. Then Todd had an idea. "Let's check for tracks coming out of the woods!"

Everyone agreed. At the edge of the woods, they found deer tracks heading towards Blake's cabin. But it looked as if the deer had turned back around for some reason.

It was a mystery! The four friends sat down in the screened-in porch at Maria's cabin. As they chatted, Blake picked up a magazine that sat in a basket near his chair. It had articles about outdoor sports.

As Blake flipped through the pages, one article caught his eye. He read it quickly.

"I've got it!" he said. "I bet I know why the deer have been staying away! Follow me!"

In seconds the friends were standing in Blake's yard, between their lawn-chair goal posts.

"What's the one thing you notice in this yard that isn't in any of the others?" Blake asked.

The three kids looked around. "Just your sweatshirt on the chair," Maria said finally. It had been lying there since their very first soccer game.

"Right!" Blake said. "I just read this article that said deer have a really good sense of smell. It said hunters spray their clothes with something that covers up human scent, because deer run away when they smell people."

"So you think your sweatshirt was keeping the deer away from your yard?" Nicholas asked.

"That's what we're going to find out," Blake said, grabbing his sweatshirt. "Let's see what happens tonight. Everyone come over after dinner."

That evening a soft rustling sounded just beyond Blake's cabin. The four friends were ready and waiting at the sliding glass door. As they watched, two deer and a fawn made their way delicately across the shadowy backyard. They paused to nibble on fresh apples Blake had put out for them.

"You were right!" Maria whispered.

Blake smiled, satisfied at last. "I'd say the case of the missing deer is finally solved!"

Encounter

By Lilian Moore

We both stood
heart-stopping
still,

I in the doorway
the deer
near
the old apple tree,

he
muscle wary
straining
to hear

I holding breath
to say
do not fear.

In the silence
between us
my thought said
Stay!

Did it snap
like a twig?
He rose on a curve
and fled.

Deep in the Forest

By Barbara Juster Esbensen

Deep in the forest
curled in its grassy
bed
the fawn
lies
dappled with circles
lies
hidden under
medallions of sunlight
and woodland gloom
almost invisible

YOU CHOOSE THE ENDING

In "The Case of the Missing Deer," a tossed sweatshirt foreshadows the deer staying away from Blake's cabin. In the story below, events also foreshadow future events. Read to decide which ending makes the most sense—or create your own ending.

THE MISSING REPORT MYSTERY

It was Laura's birthday, but she wasn't happy. All weekend she had worked hard on a science report about woodland habitats. Now it was missing.

"It's the best report I've ever written," Laura moaned, looking down at her family's new puppy.

"Come with me, Rusty," she said. "Let's look for my report." Rusty wagged his tail and dropped the newspaper he'd been chewing on.

Laura led Rusty from room to room.

"Have you seen my report?" Laura asked her sister Paige, who was sitting at the kitchen table. Paige quickly slid something under a placemat.

"Report?" she asked. "What report?"

Ending 1: Laura finds her report in the living room, chewed to pieces by Rusty. Paige had been making a surprise birthday card for Laura.

Ending 2: Rusty leads Laura to the report, which he had carried in his mouth to her school.

Ending 3: Paige hid Laura's report, so she could surprise her by making a drawing for its cover.

WHO DID IT?

After reading "Fossil Fish Found!," you know that a few people were involved in the 1938 discovery of the coelacanth. The main ones were:

- **A.** Dr. Smith
- **B.** Ms. Courtenay-Latimer
- **C.** The captain of the *Nerine* fishing boat

Read each of the six statements below. Which person above does each statement best correspond to? On a separate sheet of paper, match each statement to a person by writing the number and letter that go together.

- **1.** First to see the strange fish
- **2.** Thought the fish might be a coelacanth
- **3.** First to contact Dr. Smith about the fish
- **4.** Offered a reward for more coelacanths
- **5.** Was bitten by the strange fish
- **6.** Had the strange fish stuffed

Writing to Remember

For centuries people have been writing down their experiences in diaries and journals. Journals have opened a window on what life was like in many different times and places.

A journal entry can be a good way to help you write a personal narrative about an experience. For example, in "The Case of the Missing Deer," Blake might have written about his excitement at seeing the doe and fawn.

Write your own personal narrative. Think about a discovery you have made, and write a journal entry about it. It can be a place you have visited, something you've done for the first time, or something you've observed in nature. It can also be a fictional discovery—a place you imagine seeing or an activity you imagine doing.

Write the date for your journal entry. Record your thoughts, feelings, and what you saw, heard, and did on this particular day. Include details. Write so that someone reading your journal will understand something about you and the world you are writing about. If you like, include small drawings that relate to your writing.

May 25

Today was a momentous day. I saw a bald eagle for the first time. It was perched in a tree at the edge of the lake.

Journey to Cuzco:
The Origin of the Inca

The Incan empire of South America was once the largest empire in the Americas. It stretched through the Andes mountain range from present-day Colombia to Chile. The Inca's great skill in farming and building can be seen in the ruins of Machu Picchu (MAH choo PEE choo), near Cuzco (KOOS koh), Peru.

The following ancient myth tells about the origin of the Incan civilization.

Machu Picchu lies on a mountain ridge about 8,000 feet high.

Viracuchu (veer uh KOO choo), the sky god, saw that the night sky was empty. So he created the moon, the stars, and the planets.

Viracuchu's son was Inti (IHN tee), the god of the sun. Inti felt that people needed order in their lives. On a lake in the Andes, he created the first Incan people. They were Manco Capac (MAHN koh KAH pahk) and his sister, Mama Ocllo (MAH mah OHK yo). Inti sent them on a journey. Their mission was to find the place for the Incan civilization to begin.

How would Manco Capac and Mama Ocllo know when they had found the right spot? Inti had given them a golden staff. The chosen place would be where the staff sank deep into the earth.

The brother and sister journeyed into the bitterly cold Andes Mountains. They traveled through underground caves. At times they discovered hidden valleys. At each location, they tested the ground. It was always too hard; the golden staff would not go through.

Finally, the travelers came upon the most beautiful valley they had seen. When they tried the staff, it went so deep into the earth that it disappeared. They knew they had arrived. The site became Cuzco, the first capital of the Incan empire.

Manco Capac and Mama Ocllo taught men and women to farm and build houses, to weave cloth and to prepare food. From these humble beginnings, the great civilization of the Inca developed, with Manco Capac as its first emperor.

Manco Capac

After you read the myth, describe how it explains the origins of people, places, and phenomena in nature.

Get Lost!
The Puzzle of Mazes

Getting through a maze can be a challenge!

Imagine you are running along a narrow, gravel pathway. On either side of you is a six-foot wall of tangled hedges. Openings along the hedge lead to other long, leafy green hallways. They all look the same. You are caught in a maze! Can you find your way out? Even a compass won't help you. Many of these twisting passageways will never take you to the end. Instead, they lead to dead ends and you have to retrace your steps. This is what makes mazes so much fun—and so difficult!

What's a Labyrinth?

Many people confuse mazes with labyrinths. Unlike mazes, many labyrinths have no walls at all. They are simply designs built into a floor or other flat surface. Mazes are multi-cursal, meaning they have many paths. A labyrinth is unicursal—it has a single path from the beginning to the end. Most labyrinths are less challenging than mazes, but there's one exception you'll read about on page 73!

Hemmed In by Hedges

Hedge mazes are one of the most common kinds of mazes. These are often made from the yew, an evergreen tree or shrub. Yews make good maze borders because they grow slowly and keep their shape.

Mazes are created in all kinds of designs from easy to difficult. Some mazes end in their middle. In others, you must find your way from one side to another. In 1977, Queen Elizabeth celebrated twenty-five years as queen of England. To mark this event, brothers Edward and Lindsay Heyes created the Silver Jubilee maze.

The slow-growing yew tree

This "aMazing Hedge Puzzle," as the brothers call it, has twelve paths to the center and thirteen unlucky dead ends. And there's a balcony outside the maze from which you can shout hints to your friends inside—or confuse them even more!

The Silver Jubilee maze pathways can hold many people at once, and even wheelchairs. So many people visit that the paths wear down two inches a year!

The length of mazes can vary, too. Some are extremely long. In 1975, for example, Greg Bright created the Longleat Hedge Maze in Wiltshire, England. This maze, one of the longest hedge mazes in the world, uses more than 16,000 English yew trees. It takes about ninety minutes to complete. Other mazes are short and may take very little time to finish.

The Longleat Hedge Maze has almost two miles of pathways.

A Royal Puzzle

One of the most unusual hedge mazes is found at Leeds Castle in Kent, England. Made from yew and designed by a maze expert, it was planted in 1988. Part of the maze is cut in the shape of a crown to honor the many queens who have lived in the castle. At the center of the Leeds Castle maze is the entrance to a grotto, or cavern, filled with sculptures of mythical beasts.

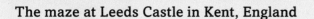

The maze at Leeds Castle in Kent, England

If you're lucky enough to find your way to the center, you can climb to the top of a small tower for a view of the entire maze. Then you can take stone steps down into the most unique part of the maze—its grotto. The maze winds through an underground cave that's cold, dark, and narrow. This part of the maze is unicursal, which means it has a single path leading from the beginning to the end. You can't get lost!

Can you find the crown in the maze?

If you find your way to the center tower, you will have the chance to explore the underground part of the Leeds maze.

For younger children, Leeds Castle offers the Turf Maze. No taller than ankle height, this maze also has a surprise at its center—a small wooden castle. Leeds Castle offers something to amaze both the young and the old.

Even young children enjoy the maze experience at Leeds Castle.

Underground you will pass a fountain carved in the shape of a mysterious face. Follow the light to the end of the maze!

Lost in the Cornstalks

There are hedge mazes in the United States, but not as many as in England. Our most common type of maze is made from cornstalks. It's nicknamed a maize maze because maize is another word for corn.

Unlike hedge mazes, which last for years, maize mazes last for only one season. However, they are fast and easy to grow. Designs are usually cut into the cornfield with tractors when the corn is only a few inches high. Picture designs are especially popular for maize mazes. And since corn is tallest in the fall, these designs are often related to the season of autumn.

Maize mazes are fun but hot and dusty inside. Be sure to bring water and wear running shoes instead of sandals when you try one!

Not all maize mazes have autumn themes. In 1993, British maze designer Adrian Fisher created a huge corn maze in the shape of a dinosaur in Harrisburg, Pennsylvania. Other maize mazes have featured castles, a map of the United States, an Egyptian pyramid, the Statue of Liberty, a cowboy, a pig, and even a portrait of the actor John Wayne.

Corn mazes are created in all kinds of imaginative designs!

A Test of Skill

Have you ever tried making your way through a maze on paper? If so, you know you place your pencil at "Start" and draw a line all the way through to the end. If you practice solving paper mazes, it might help you find your way through a hedge or maize maze. You may not need to go very far to try. Mazes have become popular tourist attractions, and they're found all over the world. Maybe you'll get a chance to test your maze-solving skills outdoors. Good luck!

Labyrinth of the Minotaur

A story from Greek mythology has made one labyrinth famous the world over. In ancient days, King Minos ruled the island of Crete where people lived in fear of a beast called the Minotaur. The Minotaur had the head of a bull and the body of a man.

Minos kept the Minotaur in a huge labyrinth. Every few years fourteen people were sacrificed to the Minotaur. But Theseus, a brave young man, volunteered to stop this terrible practice by battling the Minotaur.

King Minos' daughter, Ariadne, gave Theseus a sword to fight the Minotaur and a ball of string to help him find his way out of the labyrinth. Theseus killed the Minotaur, rescued the people who were meant to be victims, and led them out to freedom.

"Minotaur Waking," a bronze sculpture by Michael Ayrton

The Best Paths

by Kristine O'Connell George

The best paths
are whispers
in the grass,
a bent twig,
a token, a hint,
easily missed.

The best paths
hide themselves
until the right
someone
comes along.

The best paths
lead you
to where
you didn't know
you wanted to go.

compass

by Valerie Worth

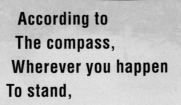

According to
The compass,
Wherever you happen
To stand,

North, south,
East and west,
Meet in the palm
Of your hand.

Grand Opening

MAY'S MAZES

DISCOVER THE TIGER HEDGE MAZE!

- Find your way to the giant tiger in the center!
- Twenty dead ends and only one right path!

STROLL THE LAKESIDE LABYRINTH!

- Music from hidden speakers!
- Dancing fountains!

TRY MAY'S MAIZE MAZE!

- Cornstalks twelve feet tall!
- Clue sheets for the confused!

Read the above ad. Discuss with a partner how it presents its message differently than an online ad or a TV commercial might. Then test your memory. Cover the ad and read the list of details on the right. Tell which maze each one goes with.

Twenty dead ends! _____?_____
Dancing fountains! _____?_____
Clue sheets! _____?_____
Hidden speakers! _____?_____
Giant tiger! _____?_____
Cornstalks! _____?_____

A-maze Yourself!

You don't need a cornfield or hedge paths to make a maze. Here are instructions to help you make your own maze at home or in class.

Materials:

Pencil, paper, and eraser

Step 1 Draw a large rectangle for the frame of the maze. Use the diagram on this page as a guide. Mark where you want your maze to start (S) and finish (F).

Step 2 Start making your paths. Make horizontal lines and vertical lines to turn your path in different directions. Put a line across your path to make a dead end.

Step 3 After you have finished your maze, try to solve it. You may need to close off some paths or open others.

Extras

- Make your maze in the shape of an object or animal.

- Draw little pictures or write messages by the paths.

A Writer's TREASURE

A treasure is waiting to be found, but only you know where it is hidden! How can you help someone find it? First, on a separate sheet of paper, write a sentence that tells what the treasure is and where the seeker needs to go. (It could be anywhere—in a Chinese forest, a fictional island, or in your own house.)

Next, write instructions for finding the treasure. Is it buried underground, tucked in a hollow log, or hidden in an attic? Wherever it is, choose a starting point and write step-by-step instructions that will lead someone to the hiding place. Include clear details—landmarks and site markers—in your instructions. Add a few directions that will require using a compass, too.

Finally, you can also draw a simple map to go with the instructions.

Here is an example.

MAP

Treasure
Oak

Village of
Coolhead

Fern
Hill

Fern Park

Island of Bells

Village of
Hot Foot

N

W

E

S

The treasure is three golden coins.

You will need to travel to the Island of Bells.

1. Go to Fern Park in the village of Coolhead.

2. Walk to the twisted oak tree. Look in the hollow for a key.

3. Walk east for 45 steps.

4. Look for a blue rock.

5. Dig under the rock exactly three feet.

6. Find the green metal box and use the key!

Credits